Garden

No part of this publication may be reproduced, stored in or introduced into a retrieval system, or transmitted, in any form or by any means (electronically, mechanical, photocopying, recording or otherwise), without the prior written permission of both the copyright owner and the publisher of this book. Re-selling through electronic outlets (like Amazon, Barnes and Noble or eBay) without permission of the publisher is illegal and punishable by law. The scanning, uploading, and distribution of this book via the Internet or via any other means without the permission of the publisher is illegal and punishable by law. Please purchase only authorized editions and do not participate in or encourage electronic piracy of copyrightable materials.
Your support of the author's right is appreciated.

Edited by Lorraine Fortier

Cover Design by Del Hall IV

Cover Image by Valentyn Volkov courtesy of shutterstock.com

This book is a F.U.N. Inc. publication, the parent company of Guidance for a Better Life retreat center.

www.guidanceforabetterlife.com

Copyright © 2024 F.U.N. Inc.
All rights reserved.

ISBN: 978-1-947255-97-5

GOD
IS IN THE
Garden

PARABLES
BY DEL HALL IV

PAR'ABLE, *noun* A fable or allegorical relation or representation of something real in life or nature, from which a moral is drawn for instruction ...

(Websters 1828 Dictionary)

Table of Contents

Welcome 1

The Garden 3

There is More 8

Poplar Rock 12

Tomato Salad 19

Zoe's Shovel 24

Grow What You Love 29

Free Will 33

Grafting On 37

Pruning 42

Easter Gift 47

The Woodshop 51

Level Up 60

Show Me Love 68

Love Conquers All 77

Fear is a Condenser 84

Bee Love 90

Nurture the Roots 97

Cut Your Own 102

Under the Hood 107

Stay Open 111

The Sandbox 115

The Rim 120

Surrendered to the Echinacea 124

Until we Meet Again 126

Welcome

Contained within the following pages are twenty-three parables. Most of them are inspired from my family's journey onto the mountain and into the grand adventure of homesteading and all that it entailed: clearing a home site, building a house, planting a garden and orchard, keeping bees, raising chickens, and so forth. I learned so much along the way and was constantly amazed at the perfection of the situation — even during the times when things didn't work out as I had planned. It always makes my heart smile to be shown a deeper lesson about the nature of God, myself, and life through the everyday events of living. This includes my time spent in the garden of course, and I am so pleased to be able to share them with you now. I hope you will see past the surface value of the stories and benefit from their deeper meanings.

It is also my hope this book will serve as a memoir for my family. At the time of this writing two of our three daughters have grown and moved out, and it won't be long before the third follows suit. This is the nature of things. Writing these stories brought back many memories for me, way more than actually made the final book. Down here in these physical worlds of matter and space, time waits for no one. It constantly flows on, without pause. I try to live in the moment the best I can, but one must also plan for the future and occasionally reflect on the past. These parables help me to count my blessings of the wonderful time I had with family, my wife, and three wonderful daughters on the mountain. It was a blessed experience! And who knows ... life is long and you never know what it will bring. Perhaps we will find ourselves again together on the mountain someday.

For everyone else reading perhaps join me on the mountain in your hearts. If you take some of what I learned and go deeper with it, your life could be transformed for the better. Ultimately, I hope this book is a blessing to you in some way ... and remember — you are loved and you are not alone! Nor are you forgotten.

The Garden

At the time my wife and I were raising our three daughters we were blessed with the opportunity to have room for a large garden and orchard. It was a lot of work but as anyone who is borderline obsessed with something they know it's best to say "It was a labor of love." I initially drew out plans to scale on a very large sheet of graph paper spending hours penciling in and erasing various layouts looking for the most effective and efficient use of the space — as well as one that would make my heart sing – the biggest reward of gardening. Yes of course, there are many rewards to gardening comprised of countless small moments: successful harvests, time spent together with family, tasty fresh meals, satisfying views of weeded and strawed beds, that fifteen minutes we call "glow-thirty" right when the sun has almost set and everything takes on an almost warm glow as if everything is lit from the inside – even the air itself seems to vibrate with light — well-enjoyed fresh veggies and the like, but what does it all boil down to? They are all moments that open my heart. Let me slow down and say that again because it's very important. They are all moments that open my heart. That is the true reward of gardening for me — it opens my heart and an open heart is the key to everything good in life. More on that later. Much more.

That's not to say every second I was in the garden I was joyfully floating around like Mary Poppins, but the idea of this point is to focus on the wins. Somedays the hot sweaty mess I was and the seemingly endless cloud of gnats hovering around my head took the win. No sense in being naïve when it comes to anything — especially working with and within the confines of the Earth — some days it's tough and your heart is less open. Learning to cultivate an attitude of gratitude and recognize and take the time to appreciate the days and moments when it is open and things do come together is crucial. There are so many, what some would classify as small things, to be grateful for. The fruit tree blossoms making it through spring without a late frost would be just one example. They are absolutely gorgeous to behold and they smell absolutely divine. Closing your eyes and mouth and breathing in deeply through your nose their glorious sweetness, gazing at the purity of their bright white and pink beauty during peak bloom, and then enjoying the flower petal drop encompass you as they drift through the air like gentle snow falling. I've learned to cherish the few weeks when our thirty or so heirloom apple trees are blooming regardless of if they yield a single apple or not. This spring "snowfall" is glorious. Watching the honey bees navigate their way exquisitely through the petals raining down as they themselves are weighted with a victorious load of pollen is magnificent. One of the biggest lessons gardening has taught me is to enjoy where I am at right here — right now, in this moment. It's okay to reflect on the past and plan for the future but it's here in the NOW where I try and dwell.

So where was I? Labor of love — yes. Gardening and tending to our small orchard have provided many moments of joy. It has also taught me many things about life and has given me revelations into how God works. I think it's amazing how the Heavenly Father can use what we each love to teach us His ways and His truths and bless us with insights to help guide us on our journey through our daily walk and ultimately home to Him. We simply need to learn how He speaks to us and be willing to listen. He loves us enough to "speak" to us in a way that we will be able to "hear" Him. He can also use the things going on in our daily lives that perhaps don't make our hearts sing to get a message through to us. Our challenges are often our greatest opportunities for spiritual growth.

We are each spiritual beings in temporal bodies, or what I like to call an "Earth-suit," but at our core we are eternal spiritual beings. As such — we need love. We need to receive it and we need to give it. It's that simple. That's a huge part of the reason we are on Earth — to learn to give and receive love. This is a lot easier to do if our hearts are open. Not literally open of course but receptive to love. Lifted up ... moved ... touched ... receptive. What is it that makes your heart smile? What opens your heart? Hopefully, many things. For me one thing is sowing seeds and dreaming and tending and hoping. As anyone in the same situation knows it's best to find the joy in the process of gardening and spending the time planning and dreaming rather than in just the harvesting. If the harvest is all you're after then gardening can be a bit of a different story due to the multitude of obstacles between you and your garden-fresh meal. There are just too many potential things between you and that gardening magazine cover shot. These words are in no way meant to discourage. You can do it! You will have your successes! But you'll ultimately have more joy in the experience if you focus on enjoying the process too, not just the end goal.

Not all the parables in this book are stories from the garden, but most are, and it made my heart smile to use them so I did. It's my hope you'll be inspired to see the Hand of God in your own life through them — whether in the garden or wherever you may find yourself.

There is More

When I was growing up the choices for apples were simple — Red Delicious or Golden Delicious. But I came to the conclusion very early on there was nothing delicious about them, especially the Red Delicious. It was not until years later I came to learn they were not grown for flavor but for their ability to be picked early, shipped across the country, and still look pretty on the shelf. Flavor was not the highest consideration.

Even though my experience with apples available on the supermarket shelf did not reflect it, somewhere deep inside I knew it was a good fruit. I had faith there must be more to the apple; how could there not be? For the most part they served their purpose, but they still felt hollow to me, a shell of their true glorious potential. Looking back, I do not even remember if I believed there was a good apple out there somewhere, but I knew what I currently had was lacking something.

Life can be like this for many. On the surface it is good or perhaps even great. They have a good job, a loving family, hobbies, friends, a nice house, enjoyable vacations, fellowship at church, a belief in God, and there can be genuine joy in all of it. But still, something nibbles at them. It is the feeling that there is more. What is it they are missing? It is not a negative judgment of our current lives to consider there could be more. There is always more! Our life can be even more abundant. Always and in all ways. There is almost no limit to the amount of joy that can be brought into our lives.

Somewhere along the way stores started carrying Granny Smith, Gala, and Fuji. I am sure I recognized this as an improvement to the state of the apple, yet it still did not fill the void. Something was still lacking. The apple had still not manifested its highest potential in my life. Years later my family and I were driving down a country road in Virginia and came across an orchard and packing shed that specialized in heirloom Virginia apples. I'm not even sure how I ended up there, but I still remember it vividly. I walked up to a table with cases of apple varieties I had never heard of before. Apples of all shapes, sizes, colors, and textures. The owner came out and I began excitedly picking his brain with all sorts of questions. It turns out they had over two hundred varieties of apples that you cannot get at your local store. This in itself blew my mind as I could probably only list a dozen varieties I had previously heard of. Many of the apples on the table before me were grown in the orchards of our founding fathers, which touched me on many levels.

The owner took out his pocket knife and sliced off pieces of one after another after another for us to try. As he handed them to me I could feel his joy in being able to share them; he knew what it was he was offering. I sampled dozens of phenomenal apples that afternoon with a variety and depth of flavor that was absolutely incredible. When I eventually left for home my heart was as full of gratitude and contentment as the car was loaded with paper bags full of newly discovered treasure.

When I was sampling apples that day it literally almost brought me to tears. In retrospect it wasn't so much the flavors that moved me. It was the "knowing" that I had been carrying all these years that there was more to the apple had been proven to be true. At this point in my life I had probably even forgotten this knowing I carried, but when I tasted these flavors it all came back. There was more! My heart knew it and here it was, right in front of me. I had faith the apple was indeed a good fruit. After all these years here was the proof, and how sweet it was!

I share this story because it is my hope this book could be like my trip to the orchard for some of you. I hope the truths contained within these stories of my journey onto the mountain and into the garden and orchard help you solidify what your heart already knows. There is more to life; deep down you know there is. You are more than just your physical body; you are an eternal spiritual being created out of the Light and Love of God. God loves you and you are not alone, nor are you forgotten. God always has someone here on Earth to help show you the way home to Him.

Poplar Rock

Before my father rented heavy equipment so we could do the final tidying up of my future homesite, field, garden, and orchard, I spent the better part of three years on and off clearing with a chainsaw, making piles of logs for firewood, and brush piles to burn in the winter. Mostly trying to establish a foothold and get some breathing room. It had been a long time since much had been done with the part of the property where I wanted to build and as a result, it was now in the chokehold of grapevines, broken trees, brambles, and the like. Cutting out this small stuff to free some of the large poplar trees was quite satisfying. The big beautiful trees were there — ready to shine and be seen, but they just needed a little help getting unburied. They were presently at the point where they could not do it alone. An intervention of sorts was needed. Thankfully I had a chainsaw and the energy and motivation to get in there and free them. It was always so satisfying to clear the brush up to and around one on all sides that I had decided to keep and mark it with bright orange flagging tape. It was like claiming it — like *This one's mine — back off brambles — I'm going to look after it.* Almost like taking a sheep into the fold. At one point or another we could all use a little help.

During this time of clearing a spot for my future homesite and dreaming of the day I would build a house on it I also played with the idea of a name for the homestead. It would be a small piece within my father's property, but it seemed like a fun idea to name the roughly four to five-acre spot we'd be tending to and calling home. The name Poplar Forest came to me very early on and I was quite pleased with it. It seemed very fitting. It was literally a forest of very large poplar trees. So there it was, name picked, major decision taken care of, time to move on with the clearing and the dreaming and the building of our mountaintop home — so I did.

On the mountaintop we have quite a few varieties of trees: maples, oaks, black walnuts, pines, sassafras, birch, and many many more. They all have unique qualities that make them each special in their own right but my personal favorite is the tulip poplar — or simply poplar. Funny thing is for quite some time I didn't realize they actually had full-size tulip flowers on them in the spring and early summer. Guess it sort of makes sense with a name like tulip poplar. I absolutely love them. They're such beautiful stately trees. They grow tall and true and can weather the storms up here. I have seen them yield branches to an ice storm but never have I seen a whole tree toppled over with the root ball in the air. They seem to have learned how to give up the small losses and stay in the game rather than holding on so tight they lose everything. They grow very tall and straight in a race for the light and stand like pillars or old temple columns. I love being surrounded by them in the woods around our house. If grown in more open areas they will branch out more, filling the space around themselves more efficiently. I suppose most trees do this but I notice it more with the poplars.

A couple years after we moved to the mountain I was at the Monticello Visitor Center and they had one of those huge racks with information on hundreds of local attractions. One caught my eye and I could have sworn it said Poplar Forest but the name was partially blocked. I asked if I could have one and when it was handed to me I couldn't believe it. Poplar Forest was the name Thomas Jefferson gave to his second home. Name already taken. Figures. Back to the drawing board for me and eventually to the name Poplar Rock. We have plenty of rocks on the mountain too. It wasn't the Poplar Forest I had been carrying for a couple years but in hindsight, I couldn't imagine a better name for the homesite. There was only one small problem. Not really a problem, but a small glitch. When you're approaching our house on the gravel road it curves to the right and as the clearing begins, with the house now in sight, there is a huge boulder on the right side of the road with a large black walnut tree leaning right up next to it. The tree literally has a curve in it to accommodate the shape of the car-sized rock it has probably been growing next to for years. See the glitch? I have my rock but no poplar. Had I nicknamed the place Black Walnut Rock I would have been golden but alas I did not.

So in the grand scheme of things not really a big deal. Not really even a small deal yet it took the teeny, tiniest little bit of my peace every time I drove by it. I'd think *Man I wish that was a poplar tree next to the big rock — it'd be perfect Poplar Rock.* I'm slightly embarrassed to say this went on and off for years. I'd lose a tiny bit of peace over that tree not being a poplar tree. The thing is those tiny bits of peace we give up accumulate. Sometimes we may not think they are worth dialing in but they are because like I said they add up. You give away a little bit of peace on ten different things and before you know it your heart is closing and you are less receptive to the Holy Spirit. The heart is how we "hear," and it's a snowball effect, so the little stuff does matter. Finally taking that to heart as I drove in late one night I stopped the truck and just paused with my headlights beaming onto the rock and black walnut tree and I truly surrendered it. I let it go. I let my attachment to the way I wanted it to be go and just trusted God that it was the way it was supposed to be. This in itself brought great comfort and that is the beauty of surrender. It takes the weight off of us — we don't have to carry the worry or the attachment or the fear or whatever it is. If we can truly hand, whatever it is, over to the Divine, "Let go and let God" as many say, it will release you and it truly did. After a few moments of true surrender and reflection, I continued on to my house and went to bed with deep peace in my heart. Was I in for a surprise when I woke up the very next morning.

Shaking the sleep from my hair the next morning and gazing out the window I did a doubletake. That huge boulder had moved from where it had been for years on the side of the road and it was now sitting dead center in the middle of the gravel road. It took me a few moments to even process what I was looking at before I even had time to think about what and how it had happened. Eventually my eyes and brain started working together and came to the realization that yes indeed, that was a huge rock in the road. Very shortly after that I realized the rock was the huge boulder that was part of my surrender from the night before. During all these realizations of the physical and the mind, Soul just smiled. It knew what was going on. I had truly surrendered the situation and was no longer going to allow it to chisel away at my peace and God knew I was for real about it, and since I had grown in surrender the boulder could now go just about anywhere. Speaking of which. That very day a heavy equipment operator was bringing a huge track loader to the property to begin on a different project and I was able to borrow him for ten minutes to move the rock out of the road. The speed with which God responded to my true surrender still blows me away. I drove past that black walnut and rock for probably five years and it was less than twelve hours from the time of my late-night surrender till a track loader was coming up my driveway to move the rock out of the road, and the operator asking me "Where do you want me to put it?"

"Right next to that poplar tree please."

Tomato Salad

One of the first times I ever grew green beans I built a really nice structure out of saplings which I tied together with twine after pushing one of the ends into the ground. I would slightly crisscross them as their bends and nuances allowed, creating essentially a vertical fence. It was very beautiful to me, and it was important to provide something for the beans to climb as they grew. Constructing and then eventually seeing vegetables on garden structures is one of those many small things about gardening that brings me joy and opens my heart. In future years as our fruit trees grew in size I was able to use their branches from when I pruned the trees back in early spring to weave together a fence for the beans to grow up. This to me was even more satisfying.

It's a good thing the wooden structure I built was pleasant to look at and didn't need to be hidden by beans because it was visible all season. A resting post for weary birds and a reminder of one of many early gardening fails. But one that would not be repeated. I like to learn from my mistakes — it makes them tolerable. It turns them into learning opportunities. And what was that mistake? Well apparently there are two categories of beans each containing many varieties, bush beans and pole beans. One is a bush and one is a vine that climbs. You can probably guess which type I had planted next to my trellis, yep ... bush. Fail. Not sure if I grabbed the wrong pack or if I was even aware at the time that there was a difference. Sounds very obvious to me now.

Another solid "win" in my early years of gardening was — I guess we'll call it, the "baby lettuce fail." I was so hesitant to thin my crops when I first started gardening. It seemed like such a crime to pull a perfectly healthy plant that had grown because you had planted it and just toss it but you must. Two to three corn kernels or beans may go into the ground at whatever your spacing is but you have to thin it back to one once the seedlings are up. It was either the first or second year of having a garden and I had that thing jam-packed. Everything was planted too close together and nothing was thinned down to where it should have been. There is no room to be sentimental and hesitate in pulling those extra plants out. They have to go or the whole crop is lesser for it. Smaller, more susceptible to disease, crowded, and on and on. This is the present me talking, the me in the story did not thin the corn that was already planted too close together and it was like a brick of corn stalks.

This jungle of corn did provide somewhere for me to dispose of tomatoes that were rotting on the vine. The reason escapes me as to why, but I would just pitch them into the corn plot when I'd come across one in my tomato bed. Perhaps it was an early attempt at composting. During the same time I had planted a very large bed of mixed greens with the intention of harvesting them as baby greens versus whole lettuce heads. Some of you with gardening experience may know where this story is going. We had a few heavy rains after I planted the salad greens, and in the coming weeks, I started noticing "baby greens" all around the garden close to where I had planted them. I figured the lettuce seeds I had planted got washed from their beds and spread all around the garden — seemed logical. In the coming days we harvested bags full. We gave away as many as we could find homes for over the next week or two. At that point, even with my lack of experience, I started to question things and ultimately realized all the "baby greens" I had been so proudly harvesting and giving away by the bagful were baby tomato plants that had grown from the rotten tomatoes I had pitched into where the corn was growing, and the seeds washed back in by the rain. Fail … Sorry for the organic "baby greens" friends. Sometimes you just don't know what you just don't know.

Experience is a wonderful teacher and I will never do those things again. My father has said many times, something to the effect of, "If you're going to make a mistake — at least make a new one — quit making the same old mistake over and over again." If you keep making the same mistake it shows you are not learning from the experience. Another great way to avoid, or at least alleviate, this sort of trial by error is to find someone who has gardened before. It's amazing how much quicker you can progress at something when you have someone who has been there before pointing out some of the pitfalls along the way.

Everybody, including myself, has made mistakes. We've all done things we're not proud of. We've all made bad decisions and done stupid things or acted out of fear, anger, vanity, and other lower passions. It does no good to dwell on them. It's not healthy to judge your prior self by your present state of consciousness. We are all works in progress. If you're no longer doing them and you learned from them and took responsibility for them, then love yourself enough to forgive yourself and move forward. You're not that person anymore. This is a very important point because even if you have grown and are no longer doing whatever it was you considered negative, if your heart is still closed towards yourself over past thoughts and actions, it affects the quality of your life now. It affects the quality of your life, your joy, and your ability to hear the Heavenly Father's guidance which is your lifeline.

I'm a very good gardener now. It does me no good to dwell on tomato greens salad.

Zoe's Shovel

Most folks who have a home garden opt for either raised beds or the more traditional rows approach. Both have their pros and cons and there's no sense in alienating half my readers by saying their technique is less efficient or productive for whatever reason. A common thread through these parables is doing something you love in a way that opens your heart. This is because when your heart is open you have better communication with the Divine and this makes for a much smoother journey through life. So there is no sense in throwing down the "rows versus beds" gauntlet. I've done both but ultimately found more satisfaction in raised beds. They worked best for me in my garden, with my soil, so that's what I did.

Once our garden was up to its full size it had fifty-four beds. Twenty-four large four-by-eighteen-foot beds, thirty three-by-twelve-foot beds, and six four-by-ten-foot beds for herbs. Three of the twelve-foot beds, which were side by side, we gave to our daughters at some point to tend and plant as their own. I have fond memories of a kitchen table full of seed catalogs as we all thumbed through them in February each dreaming and planning our gardens with the woodburning stove keeping us warm. My wife Kate and I would help them plan but they had final say over what they would grow in their gardens. Some years they'd be packed full with every variety of vegetable imaginable and some years they would grow just a single crop, or even just flowers. We would guide them and be there to help them make their choice but ultimately it was their choice to make.

Being unique individuals and different ages they each had different interest levels and capabilities when it came to getting their beds set up in the spring and then maintaining them throughout the growing season. Some would make it through till harvest some years, some would look like a sod farm by late summer. I would shoulder the heaviest load for them in the spring and with my large spade shovel turn the beds over. An instant gratification of going from the remnants of last year's garden and regrowth of grass and weeds into a clean palette. A solid canvas of weed-free dirt. A blank canvas to manifest dreams on and paint this year's winter vision on a fresh palette of dirt. Such joy and excitement to take late winter's scribbles and seed packs and turn them into reality. Every spring was a fresh start. A chance to begin again. A time to clean out the old crops that may have failed us, or may have succeeded — either way it was time they step aside and we start again. That blank canvas of dirt was such a symbol of hope. No matter the previous year's struggles — in spring, everything begins anew. After getting the girls' beds turned and tilled up for them I'd help them plant if they wanted it. As they got older they did more and more of the whole process themselves. Each to their own measure. It gave me such joy to spend time as a family in the garden. I love all my daughters and wanted all of them to succeed at and experience the joy of gardening, but I wasn't going to force them. I'd get them set up to a good starting point and if they were interested they'd keep it going, or reach out to Dad with his big shovel if they needed a hand, but it was their choice.

At some point my eldest, Zoe, received a small spade shovel as a birthday gift from a dear friend. It was the size of a toy shovel but it was no toy — it was the real deal. Made of metal and wood and to the standards of a full-size shovel but just reduced in size down to just over two feet in length. I have purchased a few for myself in the years since and given a few as gifts. I always have one when driving the property roads on my ATV, traveling in winter, camping, pretty much all the time. It has really become indispensable — such a handy thing to have around.

She would work with her little shovel to turn the bed in spring. My shovel was bigger and I was stronger and had had more experience working the soil so I could do more and do it more quickly but it warmed my heart to have her out there next to me with that little shovel working to her measure to get that bed turned. Throughout the gardening season the beds required upkeep. It's not just a matter of planting and walking away. The trails between our beds are grass and are always creeping in on the beds. Zoe worked hard with that little shovel to keep those edges of the trails and bed clean. It motivated me to want to give her some more help if she needed it and I would find myself crisping up the edge of her bed here and there in between her maintenance of it. There is something to be said for helping someone in need. There is also something to be said for helping someone who has made the effort to help themselves to get even further.

I remember one year Zoe had completely filled her garden and I could tell she was itching to plant more. We talked it over and I said if she wanted to she could take over the bed next to her bed as well. She happily accepted so I went ahead and turned the bed next to hers. In a matter of moments her gardening real estate had doubled. It would be more work but with that responsibility came the freedom to grow more things that made her happy.

This is something you will hear again and again — with responsibility comes freedom. Heavenly Father loves us and is there for us but it makes a world of difference if we first pick up the shovel.

Grow What You Love

As a general rule of thumb pretty much anything garden-fresh tastes better to me than store-bought. Not only does it taste better but there is something deeply satisfying about eating something literally the moment after it has been picked. In a single motion from the gentle resist then release from the plant straight into your mouth. There is simply no other way to experience any fresher produce. I can't prove this and it didn't actually occur to me until I was typing this, but it's almost as if in addition to the obvious benefit flavor wise to it being vine ripe and just picked it's almost as if there are additional quantities of the life force that sustains all still residing within the morsel right at that moment of harvest that have not left it yet. Everything while alive has it. I think I'll circle back later on this topic. Certainly food for thought though.

One of our favorite vegetables to grow and eat fresh is corn. Although not literally vine to mouth in mere seconds like tomatoes, beans, or snap peas it's a pretty quick turnaround. After harvesting enough for a meal and a quick shuck they go right into a pot of boiling water. Fresh corn is so delicious. Some butter, salt, maybe pepper and it's showtime. It's one of those crops where if you have not had it "just-picked" fresh you may have a hard time imagining that it could be that much better than store-bought or even roadside stand still in their husks, yet they are. Now I'm really making myself hungry thinking about buttering, salting, wrapping the cobs in tin foil, and grilling them up.

I remember one of the years we grew corn having a "corn feast" where essentially that's all we had for dinner. We just gorged on it. We had our fill. We dined with the doors open and the gentle breeze gently moving in one, through the house, and out the other. We worked the pile down as a team one ear at a time. At one point my wife Kate said as she stared at a bare cob, "I don't know why, but I have the strongest urge to just throw this thing out the door." I said, "Well then let her rip." Hesitant at first but then with great enthusiasm she pitched that cob out the open doorway into the yard. The kids and I followed suit as we finished our ears bringing an early

Christmas to our beloved dog Dakota as it rained down cobs all over the yard from the sky above like manna from Heaven. That day we enjoyed our greatest corn feast ever. Vikings would have been proud of our vigor.

The flipside to corn is that it is a real "space hog." It takes up a massive amount of real estate in the garden. Native American cultures employed the Three Sisters technique to save space where they would grow corn, pole beans, and squash together in the same space. The beans would use the corn to grow up on and the squash would grow underneath which also shaded the soil and kept weeds down. We did this one year and it looked cool, but I didn't care for navigating the winter squash beds as I picked the beans. It occurred to me later they were growing beans for drying, and corn for grinding into meal, versus fresh eating which would all be harvested later more on par with vegetation from the winter squash dying back.

All that said in future years when we grew corn we did it in a dedicated bed. Eventually though we stopped growing it. We were glad we had tried growing it and experienced the joy of it. We truly enjoyed it, but in the end we made the conscious choice to buy it locally instead when it was in season. We know it's even better if we grow it ourselves but we are each only given so much time and energy and focus every day, and at this point it doesn't make sense to us for us to grow it. Maybe next year, maybe not — we'll see.

The thing about having a garden is that it is yours. I'm not going to come over and tell you that you are wasting the precious space in your garden growing such a "space hog" as corn when instead you could have used your space more efficiently. I am a big believer in trying to use my resources in the most efficient and effective way so as to get the most out of the blessing. There are many rewards to gardening but to me the biggest is the joy it brings. That joy opens my heart making it easier to recognize and follow the guidance of the Holy Spirit which blesses all areas of my life and all those I come in contact with. If it brings you joy to grow a space hog like corn then plant away.

Free Will

I don't remember as a young child if I ever had a fish tank. Chances are I had something but the memory is not clear. I probably came home at some point from school or a local fair to my mother's delight with a goldfish in a plastic bag "Can we please keep it?" What is clear is that when I was older I began to be drawn to large saltwater fish tank setups. I thought they were the coolest thing and dreamed that someday I would have one. With saltwater rather than freshwater tanks you have the extra element of the live corals which I found magical. Something about them takes me to another time and place. A place I normally don't get to visit. I could sit in front of one for hours watching the inhabitants of every shape, size, color, and temperament going about their daily business: corals gently doing their thing in the background within the flow, grains of sand skimming across the "seabed," splintered light from the surface of the water dancing its way all the way down to the bottom of the tank.

When the day came to actually get a fish tank I decided rather than sell a kidney I would instead go with a freshwater tank. Still a beautiful and satisfying venture but nowhere near the cost of saltwater. First things first. A lot of folks say you can't love fish like dogs and cats. Apparently you can ... it's the cuddling you won't be doing but the love is there. I learned this firsthand during the time I had a tank. Second thing I learned is that it's an active pursuit. If your plan is just to get a tank and set it in the corner because you think it looks cool but you're not fully prepared to do the work, save yourself some money and some fishes' lives now and take up something a little more hands-off. Or maybe a better choice at this point would be to start with a one-gallon tank with something simple like a beta fish before you fully dive in. A large beautiful tank requires time, effort, care, patience, focus, and constant nurturing — hopefully all done as a labor of love. The reward is in creating this thing of beauty to enjoy. We would spend hours just staring at the tank and talking instead of watching television. I didn't mind the work to keep the tank clean because it was a labor of love. When you are doing something motivated by love it makes a difference to those you are serving and to yourself. Service is truly the greatest reward. Our family enjoyed the tank for many years but when my time with fish was over for this go-around I gifted the large tank and all my gear to a young teen in town. He was pumped. I have no plans at this point to cross the bridge into the arena of becoming a saltwater tank owner. Perhaps in my next lifetime. Till then I will thoroughly enjoy anytime I get to see a nice setup.

Our time with a fish tank brought me a lot of joy and it also gave me many insights into the nature of God and how He works. One of them being free will. Those fish, whom I truly loved and did my absolute best to take care of, could go wherever they wanted whenever they wanted. They could spend their days being kind to the other fish in the tank or not. They could eat the food I provided them or choose not to. They could favor the brighter areas in the tank or stay in the shadows. They could enjoy the rocks I put in the tank for swimming around or they could choose not to. It was their free will. So in a very real sense those fish had free will to spend their lives as they pleased but there were also many things out of their control, like when a new fish was added to the tank, the quality of the water, the times when I had to change out portions of the water to keep things clean, which was needed but also was stressful, or if a filter was broken or clogged and the water quality suffered until it could be fixed. As beautiful as they are, fish tanks are a constant battleground where disease, infection, and sickness are always knocking at the door. If a tank becomes too far gone due to disease or ill fish it may simply fail or need a major shakeup to get things back on track. This sort of a reboot is way above the paygrade of the fish in the tank but it is being done for them. Everything works better in a tank if the water is clean and there are more good fish than sick fish.

Grafting On

By the time our house was finished and we were living on the mountain I had been blessed to reconnect with the apple. I knew it was indeed a good fruit after all and I wanted to be sure to make it a part of our lives. I was very grateful to have the resource of the local orchard we had been led to that day with over two hundred heirloom varieties. Since that day of original discovery we made more visits as a family, each time leaving with bags full of delicious vintage varieties of apples grown in Virginia to sample. Once home we'd slice, plate up with a label, and spread the apples out on the table for tasting and critique. These "research" trips, family tastings, along with a lot of reading on my part helped narrow down what varieties I wanted to try growing myself. I'd also pick the owner's brain every time I was there as to the pros and cons of different varieties. I probably could have answered many of my early questions myself but as I learned more and more about apples on my own in between trips my questions became more nuanced. You can always tell when someone who has knowledge on a subject by their reaction to your question, even if very subtle, whether or not it was a good one. Well, I guess in a sense there are no bad questions, but he could tell I had moved past the basics and was really interested in learning by the level of my questions. As any good teacher will do — he responded in kind. He knew I was doing my part to learn what I could on my own and it inspired him to help me go further.

Since most of these varieties are not for sale you have to graft them for yourself if you want to grow them. This entails taking a cutting from a dormant tree in late winter and storing it till spring. At this point you shorten it up and graft it onto rootstock. When I learned about rootstock it fascinated me. Basically speaking apple rootstock if planted by itself will grow into an apple tree of some sort. There is no guarantee what variety it will be nor to the quality of the fruit. It will just be some sort of apple. The way to ensure you are getting the variety you are looking for is to take a small, maybe two-inch-or-less section of the cutting (from the previous year's new growth) with two closed buds, referred to as a scion, and attach it onto the rootstock. This graft, if it takes, will heal over and become one. Whatever variety tree the cutting came from is what the tree will become. If you grafted a cutting from a Red Delicious for some insane reason onto the rootstock you would get, you got it — Red Delicious. If you grafted instead onto that exact same rootstock a cutting from the variety Golden Russet you would get a Golden Russet. If you graft a cutting from an Ashmead's Kernel you would get, you got it — an Ashmead's Kernel. The cutting determines the variety of apple which is very important but the roots play an equally important role. The rootstock determines how large the tree will be. The exact same two-inch cutting could become a thirty-five-foot full-grown tree and live, if all goes well, for one hundred or more years or a small eight-foot tree if grafted onto dwarf rootstock with a life span of maybe fifteen to twenty years. The same exact cutting. Two totally different results. There are many benefits to smaller dwarf and semi-dwarf fruit trees but when looking at size, output, the ability to survive a drought — longevity in general none come close to an apple on standard full-size roots. Plant one for your great grandkids.

I really got into this whole experience and in the end, grafted over two hundred trees. We had room for thirty or so in our orchard and some we would plant around the property. I figured I could sell the rest to fund a future project. In the end I don't think the sales amounted to much, but the journey of discovery we took as a family and joy I had in the experience was more than enough return on my investment of time and energy. Some of the trees have already succumbed to disease or overuse as a bear back scratching post but most are still standing. This year some of my absolute favorites made it past the myriad of obstacles from bloom to harvest providing enough for a small batch of fresh cider and fresh eating which we're still enjoying as of the time of this writing.

Among other things, learning about grafting and rootstock has really driven home two points for me. One — like the scion in winter storage, we may survive for a short period of time without being connected but ultimately we will wither if we are not connected to a source of true nourishment. And second — the deeper our root system the bigger we can grow and the better chance we have of making it through a tough patch — to weather the storms in life. We have a higher survivability rate, and the longer we are here, the more time we have to experience this gift of life. We also have the opportunity to provide more for others. Generally speaking, the full-size trees can produce exponentially more than the smaller trees. I have learned though to not expect a certain output based solely on the rootstock. Sometimes a tree — no matter its roots outproduces trees bigger than itself. I always leave room to be surprised.

Pruning

Learning how to prune our fruit trees as they grew was a challenge at first but I got better at it through the years. I did this through my own personal study, speaking with others who already had experience pruning, and good old trial and error. There are different approaches to shaping a tree depending on what type of tree it is, and opinions will vary on the best way to do it, but at the end of the day it's all about light. Yes there are other reasons to prune — like removing dead or diseased branches, or branches that are rubbing against each other, but the main reason when pruning a fruit tree is to maximize the light. More specifically, getting it to penetrate past the outer branches to the inner. The light is critical to not just surviving, but thriving and producing good fruit. As the orchardist it's my job to help shape them into a position to where they are best suited to receive and benefit from it. I have a pretty good picture of what a properly shaped tree should look like now but it was initially a challenge, and trees don't always react to pruning (which is what helps shape them) the same. I had seen others do it but I hadn't done it yet and here I was with all these young fruit trees trying to shape them as they grew into maturity without really having the experience to do so. Not to mention our orchard contained multiple varieties, each with a slightly different growth pattern which complicated things further. Perhaps all my research on pruning paid off or I just got lucky because looking at them now I am very pleased.

It was when I was learning how to prune apple trees that I realized branches never gravitate up the trunk as the tree grows in height. I had never really thought about it and it might sound silly to some — I can hear you laughing — but it hadn't occurred to me. At whatever height, let's say thirty inches, a branch comes horizontally off the trunk of the tree extending out at whatever angle, it will always be at that height. The tree and branch will get larger in diameter every year the tree is alive but the branch will always be at thirty inches off the ground. This ah-ha moment helped me in learning how to prune. It actually helped a lot because planning ahead for pruning a sixteen-foot tree when you've just grafted it, and it's only the size of a twig, was overwhelming. Now I knew I could reach certain benchmarks over the coming years as they grew and aim for clusters of branches, or scaffolds as they are called, at certain heights. In the meantime branches would come and go but when I reached my next scaffold height I could lock in those next three to five branches. I've found for myself that once I can "see" what I'm after when taking on a new project I can begin to see the path to get there. Even if it eventually changes or course corrects a little along the way it gets me out of neutral and moving forward.

A fruit tree can produce fruit even if it is not pruned. There are countless wild apple trees and just as many neglected home orchard trees that will testify to this, including mine some years when I was busy elsewhere. So why even bother pruning? Quality. An apple tree for example will just grow, grow, grow in every direction, basking in and making every attempt to get closer to the precious source of warmth and light raining down on it. In the process it can become very dense and full of branches, almost shrub like. The tree is perfectly healthy in some regards, soaking in the light but by growing in every which way it can block out light to the lower branches and those closest to the trunk. I've seen wild apple trees loaded with hundreds of tiny misshapen golf ball-sized apples. A feast for the wildlife but not the easiest for slicing or fresh eating. If you want your trees to produce good fruit they need good light and for that they need structure. They need pruned open areas for light and air movement. There'll also be less chance of disease in the tree and rot on the fruit if it's not a tangled mess. For someone like myself who has planted fruit trees for fruit, pruning is a must and it's actually joyful. It's such a beautiful sight for me to gaze upon my now fully grown trees in late winter or early spring, just pruned ... all freshened up. Like they have a new haircut and are ready for their first day of school which is just around the corner. Some have done better through the years and a few are no longer with me but overall it's a solid group of trees. They have the potential to produce a lot of good fruit for a long time.

Sometimes pruning can be a challenge. It can be difficult to cut things out of our lives that we have become used to, even when they no longer serve us. Like that crooked branch that's been part of that tree so long we've just kind of gotten used to it when if we really had the courage to look at it we'd see it was time to grab the handsaw and get rid of it. Is that job still right for you? Is there somewhere in your daily life you are wasting your precious gift of time? Do you still need those negative thoughts or attitudes about yourself?

I think some of the hardest things to prune are the things that have been with us the longest, but they need to go. It's ultimately for us to decide if they are blocking us from the light, and we don't have to prune alone.

Easter Gift

I really enjoyed the times over the years when we had chickens. Besides being helpful in the overall garden ecosystem they were fun to have around. Seeing them strutting back and forth, scratching here and there, and chasing after grass clippings as I passed by on the mower always made my heart smile. Something about having chickens made our little home garden seem legit. We'd tell ourselves, "We're farmers now — we have livestock," standing there surveying our yard, leaning on our shovels, chickens out hunting for bugs. The simple act of bringing some chickens into the fold gave our farm life. Obviously the plants and fruit trees did as well but something about seeing the chickens cruising around doing their thing made it seem more alive. Let's not forget about the eggs either — plenty of those to go around as well. Enough for our eldest daughter to eventually have a little side business selling eggs. At times our fridge was so full of them there was barely room for anything else — fortunately I liked eggs.

We had tried quite a few different varieties of chickens through the years, each year picking out something different. There are so many beautiful breeds of chickens and it was great fun in early winter to flip through the chicken catalogs and narrow down our selections. It was a balance between beauty and egg productivity as we made our choices but I'd say in those earlier years we favored the prettier birds. They'd definitely still lay eggs but not as many as the "plain Jane," so to say solid brown chickens. They'd be shipped directly to our post office box and the postmaster was always very keen we get down there as soon as possible to pick them up before they clucked up her office too bad. Of course we were too and it was an exciting phone call to get. We eventually did make the shift to the higher-producing chickens. Even though it was a labor of love it still took effort and at some point we all decided if the effort was going to be put into the chickens we may as well be getting the most out of it. Our daughter Zoe was in charge of the chickens at this point: letting them in and out every night (rain or shine), washing the eggs, and keeping the coop clean (with some help from Dad when things got too backed up). With the same amount of chickens she could potentially be getting over three hundred eggs per year per chicken rather than a hundred. That's a huge difference.

So brown chickens it was. And boy o boy did the eggs roll in. Now at this point if we were actual farmers who were actually trying to keep a farm afloat financially we would have also gotten rid of the older non, or lesser, egg-producing chickens. Not us though.

Not only were they beautiful to look at, these chickens had become "our girls" and an integral part of the landscape. They had tenure, so to say, and weren't going anywhere. We could have kept food costs down but what's a fifty-pound bag of feed, now and again, between friends? They were worth it — worth it for the countless day-in and day-out moments of joy they brought, and the really special ones that would sometimes come along. Not to mention all the eggs they had provided us through the years.

One spring the girls started talking about dyeing eggs for Easter. A few thoughts came to my mind — one of them was, *Our chickens lay brown eggs — not ideal for dyeing.* It may seem stubborn and it probably was, but I was thinking that the last thing I wanted to do was spend money on eggs when we had dozens of them, so many the fridge door wouldn't shut at times. I certainly would have spent the two dollars to make my girls happy but I didn't need to. Pepper, an old, old hen who laid white eggs but hadn't laid in years, dug deep and laid one egg a day for nine days in a row which provided each of our girls with three eggs to dye, and a story to remember. An Easter miracle. God hears the prayers in our hearts, whether spoken aloud or not. He certainly heard theirs and made their day, leaving us all with a story to remember. We are known, we are heard, and nothing in our life is too small for God to use to bless us with His Love.

The Woodshop

Consider yourself blessed if you have been given the "eyes to see" something that brings you happiness in life. There can obviously be more than one, but even one really good one will do, and chances are that one good one will be joined by a "friend" sooner than later because if you're doing something you love your heart is open and you become receptive to additional gifts of love. This may be peace of heart and mind, insights about the direction of your life, clarity on a decision, joy, happiness, gratitude, and on and on. Something that checks all those boxes for me is woodworking. I absolutely love it. Even now as I begin to write this parable I can feel the smile beginning to pull on my face at the mere thought of the shop, the tools, the smell of wood shavings, the process, all of it — I love it ... it's pure joy. There is such a freedom in seeing a void to fill and knowing I can do it myself — that I have the tools to make it happen. There is such a satisfaction in seeing a piece of furniture, whether a simple bookshelf or a complex hutch, go from that picture of light in the mind, to a two-dimensional drawing on graph paper (or even a simple scribble on a napkin), to a three-dimensional object in the here and now. I've found in life if you can "see" something it's that much more possible for it to actually manifest. This goes way beyond furniture and it cuts both ways. If you always have the attitude that your life is going to be rotten and that you'll never find love or improve your situation then that'll probably be the case. You have to first be able to see it and then with the right tools do your part to help manifest it.

I was taught some of the fundamental skills of woodworking, which I immediately resonated with, as a kid by my father, like using a tape measure accurately, swinging a hammer, and whatnot, but it wasn't until I was in high school that I learned how to design a piece of furniture, and it wasn't until I caught the "woodworking bug" did that happen. I remember the day very clearly. I was in art class working on a project that required six small panels that would each have a painting on them. I had a large piece of smooth thin plywood I had meticulously measured and marked for cutting down to size. My art teacher had mentioned I could take it down the hallway to the woodshop to see Mr. West and that he would be glad to cut it up for me. I kept trying to show him the marks I had made so he would know where to cut but he could care less. He simply kept repeating the question, "What size are the panels?" Eventually I told him the dimensions and in a flash he slid the rip fence of the table saw over to the measurement, locked it in once, and cut the six panels in a fraction of the time it had taken me to mark the panel. Each successive cut he made was getting farther and farther away from where I had marked, and yet they were the correct width. I had not taken into account the loss of material that occurs from the width of the blade during the cut — and why would I? I had absolutely zero experience on a table saw or any woodworking shop equipment for that matter. He handed me my panels and I headed back to art class but not before having had my eyes opened to something totally new and exciting. From that moment on I was hooked. I found many more ways to work in the need to visit the shop in the following weeks. The next semester I took a woodworking class and can still remember the look on Mr. West's face when I turned in my first assignment, which was a scaled drawing on graph paper, with a cut list, for our first simple project we were to build. His face simply said, "I've got a live one here." He taught me a lot during the remainder of my time in high school and I would go as far to say became a good friend. A few of the other students and I would often gather in the shop with him on lunch break for a meal and some good talk radio. The practical side to something like woodworking is that you can use this skill your entire life in many ways. I guess another way to say it is that it pays dividends when you learn how to do something yourself. It gives you the freedom to do it on your terms, at your timing, for a fraction of the cost. I've learned a lot in the many years since but I still think back fondly on where it began.

My current woodshop is quite small. It measures only twelve feet wide by eighteen feet long. I do dream of a larger shop someday but for the most part spend my focus making the most of what I have right here and right now. It is more than enough to get the job done. I have learned to maneuver in the small space and be efficient with my material storage and shelving. There is no heating so in the winter I allow the chippings from the jointer to fall to the floor and be spread around creating a few inches of cushion for my feet and perhaps a little insulation. Fortunately I don't use candles to light the space. In the spring it's an awakening of sorts, a pulling back of winter's covers to do a deep clean and vacuum and begin fresh after gathering enough shavings for our work with the bees. The planer and jointer shavings work wonderfully in the bee smoker. It's an interesting cycle to participate in — the cleaning out in spring and beginning anew and then by winter slowly battening up the hatches. If time allowed I could spend all day in the woodshop. It brings me such joy to see the rows of clamps all neat in a line, to feel the sawdust beneath my feet, to use a hand plane to gently take an edge off a board with one long graceful pass. If space were not a problem I would keep every one of those shavings.

They are exquisite curls of wood that make my heart smile as I see them forming up as they exit the hand plane. I stash little spheres of them in different spots around the shop knowing I can't keep them all but when I do come across one it'll give my heart a little bump. It's good to know what makes you smile inside. There are many things working against us down here to rob us of our joy and peace. It's up to us to stack the deck in our favor, whatever it may be, and in my case — wood shavings count. Know thyself. Learn what makes your heart sing and stack the deck in your favor, whether that be exquisite shavings from a hand plane, the sight of some fresh-cut flowers, the smell of bread baking in the oven, the voice of your loved one, and on and on.

Some woodshops don't produce anything, or very little, that leaves the shop. Everything that is built is built to improve the shop. A new shelf. A new table for a piece of equipment. A new cabinet, etc., etc. I too could spend a whole lifetime just building stuff for the shop because it could certainly use it, but I only have so much time every week and I'd rather make something that goes out into the world. Something that will make a difference in my or someone else's life. Yes, yes, I've previously said there is great value in doing something you love whether or not it affects anyone else or not. This is still true. But there is also something to be said for walking and chewing gum at the same time. It doesn't have to be "all" about us all the time, and in the end you'll actually come to find more satisfaction when it's not. It's good when a woodshop actually has something to show for itself, outside of itself. Funny thing about woodshops is that you never can tell by the look of one what might come out of it. A very well-equipped woodshop may produce lackluster products while a small lesser-equipped shop and carpenter may generate way higher quality furniture. You never can tell.

With woodworking the small steps add up — maintaining square is cumulative. The steps matter. Every little part of the process has value. All the measurements you make, and then retake. All the marks you make. The size of the mark you make. All the cuts. The sharpness of the blade. There are ways to become more efficient and effective in this process, but this is not the same as taking a short cut. The steps matter. Everything you do adds up and it's best to focus on the step you are on in the moment and give it your full attention. Enjoy the moment. Enjoy the step you are on. And maybe just as important is learning how to fix your mistakes because you are most certainly going to make them. You may measure that board three times and yet it still gets cut short. Short happens.

A good woodworker knows through experience not all wood reacts the same way. There is a wide range of material out there to choose from and it all responds a little differently to the milling, gluing, sanding, and staining process. Some are way harder than others requiring it to be predrilled and some softer woods almost dent from looking at them too hard. Some graciously accept stain and others would rather be painted. One is not necessarily better than the other, but it's important to know what you're working with.

Fortunately God knows us better than we even know ourselves and if we surrender to the process He will work with our grain and our knots to help us remove the excess material, which is keeping our true selves from shining like the exquisite works of beauty they already are. Crafted by our Lord, the master carpenter, with love and purpose.

Level Up

It seems like between the fear that continues to creep into our society and the ever-increased amount of time people spend staring at their phones that folks just don't talk to each other anymore. Well, at least way less than they used to. One could walk through an entire grocery store, weaving in and out of countless aisles, passing dozens of folks without making eye contact with a single one of them, let alone actually greeting them with a simple hello. I like to get crazy with it and actually engage in conversations. I know it seems insane, but it's still doable and people actually do respond — they are literally starving for it. Such a simple thing to do — taking a moment to recognize your neighbor, yet it can do so much. In some situations I've found people are more open to interacting with others. One of those is RVing. Perhaps it's because folks are on vacation and have the time to spare. Whatever the reason, it's a target-rich source of engaging with, lending a kind ear to, sharing a laugh or moment of compassion with, and recognizing a fellow

Soul. It's also a wonderful opportunity to spend quality time together as a family.

My first memories of RVing were with my grandparents in Nevada. I think I was maybe ten or twelve. They'd drop us all off and we'd tube down a river for a few hours to where they had driven ahead to set up. Once we had floated down the river and arrived at the camper we'd have a picnic, climb around on the rocks, and have other grand adventures, always with that camper as a home base for a rest or well-earned bowl of Grandma's famous macaroni salad. It really stuck with me how cool it was that we were in the middle of nowhere, beside a beautiful river with rocks to climb on and a river to swim in — yet we had the comforts of home if needed. Shade, food, AC, shelter, a restroom, etc., and at any moment we could pack it up and relocate it. The inner nomad in me loved the idea of it. It would not be until many years later that my wife Kate and I got our first camper, but I spent many years on and off traveling by other means. It's such a joy to see new places and meet new people. When I was in my mid-teens and we'd visit my grandparents I'd get to stay in the camper as my guest room and my younger sisters would stay in the house. I loved having that camper to myself to sleep in — it was like I had my own house. I don't think I was consciously thinking of it then, that if I had children someday I would want to give them the same opportunity to experience the joy of RVing, but I ultimately did get the chance, which I am very grateful for.

Years later, now married, living on the mountain, and our three girls old enough and trained up for a serious road trip, we decided to fly out West from Virginia and visit some national parks. There is so so much natural beauty contained right here within this country. On our list of places to visit: Zion, the Grand Canyon, and Bryce to name a few. I thought, what better way to introduce our ladies to the joy of RVing than to rent one for this trip. It was just over thirty feet long with a single slide-out to expand the kitchen space. It was what is called a Class C which is one of the types of RVs that are driven, not towed. The main benefit to this is the kids could have a little more freedom during transit by not being always locked in. They could sit at the kitchen table and play games, or hang out in the loft space and read while we traveled. Had we been barreling down the highway at seventy-five miles an hour this probably wouldn't have been a great idea, but we were cruising at a relaxed pace on backroads. Thinking back now — I don't remember a single seat buckle in my grandparent's rig either. It probably had one, but I certainly don't remember using it. It was a funny experience to pick up the RV from the rental place after arriving in Nevada. They showed us how to use the awning, how to extend the slide-out, and then basically said, "Have a great trip." I remember thinking something to the effect of *I'd be glad to pay a little extra for some additional training before I hit the road with this beast.* Yes, I had some memories of RVing as a child with my grandparents, but they mostly had to do with macaroni salad and campfires ... not driving one, nor any of the other countless things that needed to be done to safely operate one.

After adjusting the mirrors, some deep breathes, and fully buckling in the kids, as well as instructing them to try and refrain from making any noise even though they were very excited, I eased out onto the road, RV making so many noises that at first worried me, we headed to our first stop. Ten minutes later we triumphantly made it to our first destination, the grocery store. Our first success. A small one, but one that could be built on. I am a sponge for data and I absorbed tons on that first trip to the grocery store, as well as each successive leg of our journey. Each one built on the other, and I gained confidence I could handle it safely, which the girls were happy about because it meant they now had a little more freedom to roam the cabin as we cruised.

So here I am. I am an RVer now. That's right ... I'm driving my crew all over the Southwest, seeing some amazing sites. I've got this thing figured out. Heck — I even learned how to dump the black-water tank. I won't get into specifics, but if an RV has a bathroom in it, when you flush the toilet it doesn't magically disappear. It has to be dealt with at some point. So I'm feeling pretty good about the trip we've been on so far. We've seen some absolutely gorgeous sites, made some wonderful memories as a family, and had the opportunity to connect with many folks along the way (You know me — I love talking to strangers). I think it's maybe day nine or ten of twelve and I'm poking around underneath the camper, in a previously unexplored compartment, and I find a stack of leveling blocks. They are one-inch-thick stackable flat plastic blocks. Probably around twelve inches by twelve inches square which you drive up onto if needed. The purpose of which is to level the camper. You can use one, two, three, or none under each tire — often different amounts under each with the ultimate goal of giving the camper a level spot to drive up onto to park. It's pretty straightforward once you get the hang of it. Some sites, if paved, are already level and don't need leveling blocks, but none of the places we had been camping were. I had just been eyeballing the site and pulling in on what looked like the most level spot. It didn't even occur to me that being truly level was an option — that I could take it upon myself to improve our situation. Being new to RVing and excited about it, I can't even remember now if it bothered us, we just lived with it. We'd be prepared for the carrots or cucumbers to roll away as we chopped them and create a small blockade with the first few we cut to stop future escapees. It was something, had I known I could have done, I would have. But I do know once I realized I had the option, I never wanted to go back. When RVing now I won't stand for even the slightest bit out of level. It's subtle, but it makes a huge difference when you're out of level ... even just a little bit. You can feel it as you walk around. Everything you do — it just seems off. It affects everything — seen and unseen.

It's a lot easier to level an RV than to stay in balance in life, but it's way more important. Everything we do is affected when we are out of balance. Whether it be emotional, physical, mental, or spiritual balance. Worries, fears, negative thoughts about ourselves or others, and anger, all work against us staying in balance which diminishes our ability to see clearly and make good decisions. If we become fixated on something and can't step away for a breath of fresh air and a moment to clean the mental slate it can put us out of level. When we push too hard physically for too long and don't know when it's time to give these temporary "Earth suits" a rest it can put us out of level. When we let our emotions control us to the point of clouding what we, as Soul, our true eternal selves, know to be true it can put us out of level. Fortunately, there are many things that can help us to stay in balance — number one is staying spiritually nourished.

I've always been drawn to traveling, seeing new places, and connecting with new people, so I've found it's worth learning how to level my ride. It's better for me and my rig as well as everyone's path I cross along the way. We all could use a few "leveling blocks" — find out where you need yours. The voyage of life is much smoother and more enjoyable when you're traveling in balance and harmony.

Show Me Love

Sometimes on a clear day from the mountaintop I can hear the whistle of a freight train way far away down in the valley. That wonderful sound reminds me of a time many years ago, before I moved to the mountain. It was after I had been through a very tough patch when an opportunity presented itself for me to put some wind back in my sails. More specifically, to put some diesel in my engine to help get me back on track. This was during the time before I had met Kate, had any children, or built our mountaintop home. Not as equipped at the time to handle life's trials I took a pretty good beating on every level when the perfect storm hit — the loss of a dear loved one and another major surgery. I see no need to rehash it all as I usually find it best to heal and move on the best I can rather than dwell on times of pain and hardship. That said, sometimes once you're strong enough, having a good look at how you could have handled it better can be useful because more trials of life will come. In the case of this parable it's not necessary. I only mention it to help paint the scene for where I was "at" in life and how the opportunity for adventure that was presented to me was just what I needed.

And what was this grand adventure that was being presented to me just weeks after leaving the hospital? One that could possibly kickstart my heart and get me more focused on the joy of living again. Riding the rails — hobo style. Hopping freight trains for coast-to-coast adventures, and man did it work. It was an absolutely thrilling and adventuresome time in my life where I saw things I could have never seen by car or perhaps even on foot. I need to stop right here and add a disclaimer before I spawn a whole new generation of hobos. First off — riding freights is illegal... it's criminal trespassing and secondly it's dangerous. The ways you can get hurt or be killed are too numerous to be listed — so don't do it. Right now I feel like someone who smokes cigarettes and is telling their kids "You shouldn't smoke, it's bad for you" as they are pulling a deep drag on a butt. You have no credibility with that cigarette hanging out of your mouth. That's a little how I feel right now — absolutely no creds. I tried though. At least

I've stated the facts — it's highly dangerous, it's not legal, and I don't recommend doing it. At the time I rode trains that didn't slow me down because I was in a dark place and I saw a ray of light — the slightest twinkle of one anyways — when I heard about it from a friend who had just ridden across country from the west coast and was headed back to Oregon and was looking for a travel partner. Sometimes a little spark is all you need to get the fire going again, so I made arrangements to leave and very shortly later headed out. On paper it wasn't the smartest thing to do right after surgery but "smart" is not always the best answer. In this case it was what was best for my heart. It had a future ahead of it with lots of things to do in this life — not a one of them to be accomplished to the fullest if it wasn't fully opened. I think that goes for all of us.

There are a lot of stories I could tell from the rails but a few come to mind. The first time I was waiting to catch a train is one for sure. We were waiting in the woods, camped out for I don't remember how long — seemed like an eternity, waiting to hear the sound of an approaching train. It was on a small spur and once the train was heard we'd have time to grab our gear and get into position to catch it. I knew what the sound of a passing train sounded like but sitting there in the woods in close proximity to the tracks, I kept thinking I heard a train approaching in the distance. I kept saying "I think I hear one" ... ears strained ... hand cupped to help me hear better, but alas it would turn out to be a truck in the distance or some other vehicle or countless other things. They sure sounded like they could be one though, in the distance that would be closer and louder before we knew it. This went on for hours as we were not on a busy section of track. We heard everything — everything but a train. All I knew was I didn't want to have to resort to the dreaded "shame-train" as freight riders called the bus for those who couldn't catch an actual train. I will tell you what though — when the sound of an approaching train did eventually come there was absolutely no mistaking it or wondering! It was so over-the-top obvious. It was kind of like wondering if you were in love with someone, then when you were — you just knew ... it was so ridiculously obvious. All those "noises" that I thought might have been a train in the distance didn't even come close to when a train was actually approaching. When you know — you know. I don't remember now where that first train we caught was going but I felt an influx of joy and excitement flowing into me, stirring out some dusty areas and healing some hurts. It did not make me forget the pain of loss and the trials of life but it did allow me to get moving forward again. I saw some really gorgeous places riding freight trains — places you just can't see in a car. I've also been through some really sketchy parts of town and learned that sometimes it's best to lay low and disappear for a while.

I also made some tough calls while riding freights. Once I had connected with a great group of folks and we began traveling together. I don't remember all the places that we rode but one day as everyone was throwing their backpacks onto the train and hopping on I got the knowing, *This one is not for me.* At this point they are all on the train car, and I am still standing on the tracks looking up at their outstretched arms to help me up. Departure is imminent and I only have a few moments to get aboard. They are looking at me with confusion and I simply said, "I'm gonna catch the next one." It was a hard decision but at the same time it was an easy one because I trusted the inner guidance I was getting. I didn't need an explanation — to them or to myself. The sound of the train brake being released filled the air and my friends rolled down the track. There are definitely circumstances in life where there is strength and safety (not to mention fun) in numbers, but sometimes we still need to walk alone. Although we are never truly alone, the Holy Spirit is always with us whether recognized or not, helping to guide us through the journey of life into higher states of love. You are never alone.

I saw the Hand of God many times during my time on the rails. The one that is coming to mind now is being saved from freezing to death as I rode through northern Idaho. It was fall and I boarded a "pig train," as we called them. It was a train comprised of flatbed train cars with tractor-trailers riding "piggyback" on them. It's a beautiful open scenic ride but not a lot of room to stay out of sight other than behind the truck wheels. There is also nothing to stop the wind. You are essentially lying under a semi-truck, between the wheels, which is on a flatbed train car. The wind just rips through the space with nothing to slow it down. I was riding solo for this trip and when I boarded everything was still warm and the sun was still shining brightly. When things got dark they got cold quickly. We were barreling down the track for hours with no sign of slowing. If the train had stopped I probably would have bailed but it just barreled on into the night for hours without relenting with me more and more concerned for my actual survival and regretting more and more my poor choice of a pig train rather than something with some protection from the wind.

I had been completely covered in my sleeping bag in an attempt to not freeze to death through all of this, but even so, I was beginning to wonder if I'd make it. At my last peek out of my sleeping bag my two large bottles of water, which I had tucked in the tractor-trailer axle above my head, were completely frozen through which was impressive considering they had been shaking as we traveled down the tracks at sixty miles per hour. Curled in the darkness of my sleeping bag hurling down the rails, so cold I could barely feel any part of me I cried out "Lord, please show me love." Instantly, within the darkness of my sleeping bag, I saw a pinpoint of light in my inner vision. It grew and with it a physical warmth, brightness, and reassuring comfort. This inner light seamlessly transitioned into the physical, and I felt the tiniest ray of sunshine enter my world. I opened my sleeping bag up the size of a dime and peeked through with one eye revealing a rising sun on the distant horizon. I had survived the night. God had heard my cry and delivered me from my ignorance for the love of it. His Love filled me. It carried me through a trial and strengthened my trust in His Love and protection. It is not just there for me; it is there for all of us. I don't try and test this by knowingly making bad decisions when I can help it anymore but that said, we all still occasionally do. It's good to know we are loved nonetheless and that He is there for us.

With the sun up and a quick exit from the train yard I made my way into town — I felt as a "new man." It took my feet and legs about thirty minutes of walking to fully "thaw out" to where I could feel them. I walked, well — more accurately, hobbled, into town with such a sense of gratitude and fortification. Yes, I was happy to be alive, but even more so I was grateful that my confidence in the Lord had been strengthened. I know without a doubt God is there for His children, but it is always a blessing to be fortified in this knowing that He hears our cries, and cares enough to respond. We do not walk alone. We do not walk alone! Being reminded of this is something that will continue to pay dividends for the rest of my life, well worth the pain I endured to have that experience.

I made it to town, found a fantastic little diner, and had the most exquisite breakfast I have ever had — to this day — in my life — ever. Such joy!

Love Conquers All

For as far back as I can remember my family has always had a dog for a pet. I have distant memories of riding on my father's shoulders one night as he and my mother walked the neighborhood in the dark calling for our lost Golden Retriever, and of wrestling with her as a toddler. At the time, at my size, she seemed massive and yet I knew she loved me and would never harm me. We'd chase each other, fall down, and roll around in the grass with her smiling the whole time. It was so long ago I don't actually remember if we found her that night but she did eventually leave us for good.

I had some other great dogs growing up as well. They too came into my life for a bit and then moved on which, as any pet owner will tell you, is probably the hardest part of having one. When you lose one. It hurts so much it can make you question is it worth it. They truly become part of the family in a sense. One of the most special dogs I had ever been blessed to have was my beloved Dakota. I couldn't say enough about this girl. She was also my first dog that was not a family dog, but mine, so that added to it. Regardless — she was special. When she passed (Wow — lots of dogs passing in this parable. Hang in there folks. Happy ending coming.) it hit me harder than ever before when losing a furry friend. So hard in fact I made the decision to not have any more dogs for a while. To me it just wasn't worth it — it hurt too much, the pain of her loss was too great. I knew it was true, but I was definitely struggling with the saying "It's better to have loved and lost than never to have loved at all."

A huge part of why we are here on Earth is to learn how to more fully give and receive love. Pets can play a huge part in this journey. Knowing that but still not ready for a dog we got our two oldest daughters, who I believe were six and eight years old, kittens the next year. They were no dog, but man o man are little kittens cute. We all, myself included, had such a ball watching those little cuties do their thing. Only problem with kittens is they grow up and turn into cats. Stay with me "cat people" ... I couldn't resist. Truthfully, I don't think it's as clean-cut as you're either a cat person or a dog person. There are a lot of grey areas. I generally gravitate towards dogs but have found many cats I like, and many dogs I don't want anything to do with — so it's not a clean tidy division. Generally though I feel dogs as a whole are further along the sliding scale of demonstrating unconditional love, but like I said, it's not black and white.

Cat lovers' hard feelings hopefully averted and back to the story. So moving forward a few years and the cats are grown and doing their thing. It's becoming more and more apparent that I am allergic to them. It doesn't bother me that they are in the house, but if I pet them and then touch my eyes without washing my hands first my eyes turn red, swell, and itch. This extra effort if I want to pet and "love on" them creates more of a divide between me and the cats. We have an occasional bonding moment, but for the most part we simply co-exist in the house. That all changed one day. It's been many years and I don't remember the specifics of what led up to it but one day I was sitting on the couch with the two cats and my heart opened fully to them. Yes their "bark" was a weak "meow," they did countless destructive things in the house, and they only would accept love on their own stubborn terms, but in that moment something within me shifted and I loved them. I truly loved them regardless of the things they did that irritated me or that I considered shortcomings. I immediately poured love onto them in the form of scratches and rubs — full-blown body massages. I could see the cloud of cat hair swirling in the air around us and I knew what was coming but I kept pouring it on them and they kept soaking it up. They were in Heaven and so was I even though I knew it was just a matter of time before my eyes would be red and practically swollen shut from this massive toxic kitty dander field I had unleashed and placed myself in. Funny thing is it never happened and it never did again. From that day on I was no longer allergic to cats. My heart had shifted and my body followed suit. Never underestimate the power of love. Love for others, for family, for God, for your neighbor, and even for cats. With love anything is possible.

Speaking of love — back to dogs ... sorry, can't help taking one last shot at my cat-loving friends. A number of years had gone by since my beloved Dakota had passed and my wife was starting to "work on me" a little here and there, very gently, to start me thinking about someday getting another dog. She knew I was still carrying hurt from the loss of Dakota so didn't want to force it but she also knew what a blessing a dog would be for our family. Pets really do bring so many opportunities to learn about giving and receiving love. My eldest daughter wrote a story about the loss of her cat titled "Grateful for the Time I Had." This really is the best attitude. Cherish the time you have with loved ones and don't let loss keep you from giving it another go. I eventually started to get comfortable with the idea of another dog and then actually excited about it. Mr. Cooper as he came to be known joined us on Christmas and now I couldn't imagine life without him. He's really a part of the family as any pet should be.

No one can make the trip down to Earth without experiencing life's ups and downs. You can't have one without the other. There will be moments of great joy and there will be moments of great sadness and loss and everything in between. This is how it is in this physical world of duality. I suppose I could protect myself from the pain of losing a beloved pet by never having one to begin with but then I am also foregoing the countless moments of joy and happiness the experience brings. As much as the loss hurts I am not willing to give up the blessing of the love while they are here. This is just as true with the people in our lives. Please don't close your heart to love forever because you lost a loved one. We all need love. Even cats.

Postscript.

I love how life continually gives us an opportunity to grow — in all ways. A short time after writing this I was in a weakened state, so to say ... saddened by one of life's joyful but hard moments and as a result of this I agreed to getting my fourteen-year-old a kitten. I had said for quite a few years there would be no additional cats coming into the fold. Those that made the bus could come along for the ride but there would be no more stops. Well am I sure glad my daughter Elliot talked me into stopping to pick up this little guy for her. So much love coming and going from him it's helping me to understand cat people. I mean I learned to love fish right? And I can't even cuddle with those. Anyways — point is — there is always more. If you are open to it the Holy Spirit will continue to help you grow in your ability in giving and receiving love, and in my case — even with cats.

Fear is a Condenser

I love spending time at the ocean. I grew up at the beach and still look for opportunities to visit and vacation with family there whenever I can. For those who have never experienced the ocean for themselves I highly recommend it. There is a vastness to it that helps put perspective to oneself and to one's life. It seems to go on and on for as far as you can see and the waves never stop coming. There may be moments when it calms but it never stops, it never ceases, the waves break break break without fail. They will not relent. They will not stop. They will never fail us. A heartbeat that can never be stopped. For as long as this planet is blessed with the gift of existence those waves will continue to roll in, one after the other after the other after the other. The tide will continue to come in and go out, and the sun will continue to shine — always. Whether or not we see it is another story, but it is always shining.

I love the feel of the warm sun at the beach. Combined with some salty tight skin from a dip in the ocean and dried from the sun and gentle sea breeze, leaves my whole "Earth-suit," so to say, feeling fresh and new. If my dermatologist is reading this please believe me when I say I practice balance and don't murder my skin with too much sun — just enough to enjoy the benefits it brings physically, emotionally, and mentally. Sitting there with loved ones — my feet in the sand, gentle sea breeze blowing and the sound of the waves crashing on the shore, salty ocean air with the magnificent ocean before me is a piece of Heaven.

On a recent trip to the ocean a few jellyfish wash up on the beach in the morning and later that day a fisherman catches a decent-sized shark. I'm guessing around five feet in length. They are not fishing for sharks but occasionally one goes after their bait and they catch one. It's quite a scene as they slowly reel it in through the breaking waves, pole bent completely over seemingly ready to snap in half at any moment, as the crowd slowly gathers to investigate. After it's reeled all the way in and pulled up onto the beach, photos taken, and hook removed, it's put back into the ocean. Afterwards the crowd dissipates and everyone kind of looks at each other like *I'll just give it a few minutes before I go back in.*

The jellyfish and shark didn't keep us from enjoying the ocean for the rest of the trip but they definitely slowed us down that first day. We were a little more hesitant to go in and when we did we weren't embracing it to the fullest because we were jumpy. Every time someone touched someone's foot with their foot under water that person would practically walk on water back to shore they were moving so fast.

Fear had crept in and was making our world smaller and our joy was suffering because of it. Newsflash. Cycles of jellyfish may come and go but the sharks are always there. That said — it's a HUGE ocean. The actual chance of getting bitten by a shark is almost zero, but still — even the tiniest seed of fear can grow, spread, and reduce your freedom, ultimately restricting your world and diminishing your joy. Fear is a condenser in every way. It will make your world smaller. It will limit what you are willing to do in life, and this includes following your dreams and manifesting a life that works for you. If you are afraid to fail, or of being hurt, it becomes harder and harder to move forward as your options of success falsely seem less and less likely to come true. How much joy and happiness are we willing to forfeit by giving into fear? It's a question we can each ask ourselves and the answer may vary depending on the circumstance or the time in our life. Fear can come in many ways. Years ago I went through a very dark time, fueled by some medical concerns where my world became smaller and smaller and smaller. Fear started with the big things — it took those out first, but that didn't satisfy its hunger and it eventually trickled down to even normal daily events. It got to the point where fear had reached its long nasty arm into every aspect of my life and it truly diminished the quality of everything in it, on every level. Its appetite could not be quenched. By the Grace of God I am no longer in that dark place but by making the trip I can testify with authority the importance of this message. Do what you can to not buy into fear. Focus on love — you are loved! If you feel yourself sliding in that direction — even a little — focus on something you are grateful for. Gratitude is the secret of love and it'll help shift your heart back to love and away from fear. It's not worth doing battle with. Leave it alone and just focus on the love. Focus on gratitude. Focus on Prophet, the Comforter.

Back in the shark-infested waters on that trip to the beach. I needed something to help everyone shift their focus. Not put their "head in the sand," so to say, but to do what I just talked about and try and focus on something positive versus getting fixated on the shark sighting. That evening we picked up a new boogie board, which provided something fun to keep folks focused on, rather than a shark attack that would most likely in a thousand years never happen. The girls had long outgrown their boards from when they were little so an upgrade was in order anyways. It was actually large enough for me to enjoy as well — which I thoroughly did.

How much pain will we allow and good times will we give away by allowing fear into our hearts? It's a question we must each ask ourselves. I know for certain life is more joyful when there is less fear in it, whatever that fear may be. Do what you can to focus on love and gratitude, and Prophet can help you to find the shore.

Bee Love

Life has continually surprised me with new ways to experience joy and love. Ways I never considered. Things I never thought I'd actually feel love for, I now have. I always find this exciting when the Holy Spirit gives me the gift of another way to love. More specifically, something else to love. In this case — honey bees. I don't think in a hundred years I would have put them on a list if asked to name some things I may truly feel love for someday. Fortunately it didn't take that long because they are magnificent. My life was lacking without them, and I didn't even know it.

It made perfect sense for us to consider introducing some bees into the flock since we had so many fruit trees, which would greatly benefit from those little samurais of pollination, but also there is something truly special about locally harvested raw honey. I won't drone on about the health benefits but there are so so many. Setting up some hives wasn't the highest priority as we were establishing our mountaintop home, as there were lots of other things to be taken care of first but all the while it was on my mind. Especially in the spring when our young fruit trees were making their first attempts at blooming, or when a wild honey bee would stop in to visit a nearby dandelion. Eventually though the day came and we set about it. The first task, which had contributed to the delay in getting bees, was building a bear-proof enclosure to put the hives in. They wouldn't stand a chance out in the open. This task really was the biggest obstacle in first getting set up and going. It was basically a stout wooden frame of two-by-fours covered in welded wire fencing on all four sides as well as the top, so the bees could easily come and go as they pleased and their hives would remain safe.

In the years before their enclosure was built and we got our first bees I had read up on the art of beekeeping. There is quite a spectrum of opinion on any topic, and I like to get a good cross-section of thought before I make my initial opinion on which way to proceed. I say initial because without any actual experience it is hard to have a truly informed opinion. I did the best I could but stayed open to the possibility I would need to adjust my approach as I gained more experience. I have found books an incredible resource but they pale to actual experience and thus I allow myself the grace to change my opinion once I actually have real-world experience with something. Being overly attached to one's thoughts and opinions can really stifle one's growth — whatever the endeavor may "bee." At the time I was getting set up we were also fortunate to have the resource of a local bee supply store. I've always found it a blessing to speak to someone with real-world knowledge on a subject. This helps to balance out the often overly positive vibe I've encountered in many books. Don't get me wrong, I really value a positive attitude but without sprinkling in the occasional reality check one can be left unprepared when trials do come — and they will. I'll save us all a deep dive into hive sanitation and all the ways a hive can fail for another time. The days however of simply dropping the bees into their hive, walking away, and coming back in the fall for a bountiful harvest are over. There is just too much working against bees now. Many apiaries experience hive losses of fifty percent or more every year. Still — even with its challenges I think it's worth the effort.

I've never been the type who ran off screaming swatting vigorously at their hair when a honeybee flew by or bumped into me, but I never wanted to cuddle with them either. It was a relationship I suppose of mutual respect and distance. You stay over there and do your thing and I'll stay over here and do my thing. That all changed on the drive home after we picked up our first "package" as it's called. A small mesh container made of plastic panels with plenty of holes for air movement used to transport bees. It's usually around three pounds worth of bees which is roughly ten thousand bees — give or take a few. Also included in this package is a can of sugar water with holes in it to feed the bees during transport and a separate small wooden and wire container that holds the queen and a few workers who tend to the queen during transit. At this point the bees don't have direct access to the queen but they have time to bond with her with the hopes that once both bees and the queen are released into the hive everybody will get along. After picking up our bees and tip-toeing them back to the car we started our long drive back to the mountain.

So there we were. My wife and I, our three young daughters, and ten thousand bees. At first I had a few "what if" thoughts, involving the container lid opening and the bees filling the car and so on and so forth — you can fill in the rest ... have fun with it. But before I knew it those thoughts shifted and I said something to the bees to the effect of "You're coming home with us ladies ... I hope you like it up there on the mountain ... it's beautiful, and there are lots of flowers for you." I could feel a genuine love building for them and it began displacing any worry or low-grade fear. I started noticing they would buzz in unity and then be quiet in unity like a choir. I swore they were answering with a group "buzzzz" after we'd say "Hello ladies." I could smell them. I could sense them. I loved everything about them, and as that love quickly grew on that car ride it collapsed any remaining distance between us. I grew more and more excited to set them free to do their thing on the mountain once we got home. Since that first installment we've continued our journey with bees with varying degrees of success. There are a lot of variables at play but we tell ourselves even if we don't get any honey a particular year that our land is still better for having the bees presence. Now when working in the yard or garden if a bee stops in to say hi it's a "Hey lady — how's it going today," as well as a little smile in my heart. Often we'll just calmly sit in the grass right next to the front of the hives, bees cruising in and out right past us. So cool seeing up-close hundreds of bees coming and going. Some headed out on a new run and some returning fully loaded ready to make a pollen drop and head back out for more. Such joy they bring us. Every part of life can be improved when fear is removed, or even lessened.

Something I found really cool about bees is that every larva the queen lays has the potential to be a queen. Every single one. The only difference in whether a bee larva becomes a regular bee or a queen is the quality of their food — the level of their nourishment. All bees are fed what is called royal jelly, which is the absolute best, for the first three days and then they are fed regular honey and pollen. Future queens are fed royal jelly the entire time they are growing before they hatch — around twenty-one days. Each and every one of those eggs has the potential to be royalty and do great things. We too have the same potential if we stay nourished with and stay in our "Royal Jelly," the Holy Spirit, the Light and Sound of God.

Nurture the Roots

Unlike fruit trees, berries, grapes, and so forth where you get multiple years from a single planting, for the most part with vegetables in my temperate zone it's a fresh start every year. That is most of the crops are annuals. Corn, beans, potatoes, tomatoes, lettuce, carrots, and so forth — all the most commonly grown home garden crops will be planted in the spring or early summer, and after they've had their say and things get cold they return to the earth in the form of compost to feed future crops. Every year in the garden is a chance to begin anew with fresh beds, new plants, new seeds, and new hope. One of the only exceptions to that, which I am aware of, is asparagus.

With asparagus you plant it once and can very easily harvest crops every year for twenty or more years. The wrinkle is that it takes way more time and effort to plant the initial bed rather than simply dropping some tomato, for example, transplants into the bed. It also eliminates that bed for the rest of the season for additional plantings so it's a trade-off. Since

I had the room and we like asparagus it was an easy choice for us. Another thing that keeps some folks from planting asparagus is it takes three years before you can reap a full harvest. The first year you cut none — rather you let any asparagus that has grown from the "crowns" that you have planted grow past harvest size into what are called ferns — essentially tall airy plants. The second year you get to enjoy a small harvest over the period of maybe two weeks or so and then you stop cutting spears and allow them to grow into ferns again. This is again done with the intention of building strong roots. If you give the roots love and attention early on and build them up they will pay dividends for years and years. Speaking of which — by the third year you can harvest about as much as you can handle.

It's best to have friends and family that also love asparagus because once fully established it can be a lot. I love it but can only eat so much. Of course you could freeze, can, make soup, and so on if motivated but there is, even after the roots are fully mature, a point that you must stop harvesting spears and allow them to grow up into ferns so that they can replenish the roots for the following year. It is critical you take care of the roots. Most folks who garden appreciate garden-fresh food and the beauty of asparagus is that it fills that early slot on the vegetable availability chart. To come right out of winter and in early early spring have a delicious garden-fresh treat — for no effort (from that year anyway, other than clearing out the dead stalks from last year's ferns and putting down some fresh straw) is a solid springtime win. I love snapping off a few fistfuls, giving them a quick rinse, and then wrapping the bottom in a wet paper towel and plastic wrap. It's a joy to gift them to someone as it feels like you're handing them a bouquet of flowers.

The one thing I don't look forward to about asparagus, and even after all these years it takes me by surprise each spring the first time I eat asparagus, is what we've nicknamed "aspara-pee." That's obviously a made-up word, which is on my list of one of the simple pleasures of living — making up silly words by combining two words. My daughter Aria is also especially talented at this. Like I've mentioned before, life can be a challenge down here sometimes and if you find things that make your heart smile and bring you joy, even as simple as making up a silly word — go for it. It works for us. We've had some great ones over the years, enough to write a whole parable on.

After many many years of scratching my head in the spring after our first meal of asparagus, and asking myself what is that all about, I decided to look it up because it's incredible how fast it happens. Within fifteen minutes of a freshly harvested and enjoyed asparagus meal — there it is ... the unmistakable aroma of "aspara-pee." Apparently it happens during the metabolism of asparagus and sulfur compounds are then eliminated from your body through urine. Do not worry if you have absolutely no idea what I am talking about, or feel free to skip ahead to the next parable if I've lost you. When I looked into it I learned that not everyone has the ability to smell it — only roughly two out of three people can. Crazy thing is you can still make the smell even if you yourself can't smell it. I'm kind of torn as I type this. Would I rather not even know I was making a stink, or would I at least like to be aware of it? I think in life — I want to know where I am funking things up so I can do something about it. But with asparagus I think I'd be okay without it. That said — I'm still looking forward to next spring's harvest from an investment we made many years ago.

Cut Your Own

For as long as I can remember I have cherished the tradition of putting up and decorating a tree at Christmas time. As a young child I had three favorite ornaments that I would find a special place for and hang together on the tree. Usually set back into a cozy pocket formed by the branches. Not way back by the trunk but not dangling for their life on the end of a branch either. Just a perfect cozy private spot they could call their own but still be a part of things.

Once we had children I began to get excited about carrying on some Christmas traditions that brought me joy through the years — as well as creating some new ones. A perfect example being our annual trip to the cut-your-own Christmas tree farm, something I never did as a kid — I lived by the ocean. There may have been some, but I certainly don't remember seeing any.

Going to the cut-your-own tree farm right off the Blue Ridge Parkway was one of my favorite parts and best memories of Christmas time with the kids. It was so beautiful and such a fun family event followed by an evening of finger foods for dinner and an evening of tree decorating. We'd all head out on a beautiful drive for the tree, greeted as we'd pull off the parkway with the smell of a campfire fueled by tree trimmings, which smelt glorious for some reason, and the owner of the tree farm. I remember the first time we went there he asked if we needed a saw. I gratefully said yes and he reached down and picked up a bow saw from the pile and handed me one. It's a saw with about a two-foot blade affixed by a shallow curved "U" shaped handle. He pointed us in the direction of where we'd be picking a tree from this year and off we excitedly went. It's such a beautiful spot right on top of the Blue Ridge Mountains with clearings so you can see distant ridges and rows of trees rolling over them. The five of us strolled up and down the rows of trees as a group, then splitting up and scouting out looking for a winner, bringing back the results of their findings to the group. We analyzed as a team, looking to find that perfect tree. We knew there was one perfect for our family — all we had to do was find it. Is the height right?

Is it full all the way around? And me of course making sure it had a spot for my trio of ornaments which I still had all these years later from my childhood.

We didn't rush this process because the experience of finding the tree is half the fun versus just grabbing and going. But eventually we did and when I went to cut it boy was I in for a surprise. I'm not sure if the bow saws came from a cut-your-own rock quarry or cut-your-own metal pipe store but they were no longer fit to cut anything. I love woodworking and have done a lot of it and this was the dullest saw I have ever used. I literally checked to see if the blade was on backwards. I somehow made it happen and we did go home with a real beauty. All that said I learned from the experience and the following year I brought my own saw. Not just a handsaw either, but a chainsaw. A sharp handsaw would have done just fine but I wasn't messing around. As we strolled the rows of trees that year I noticed people fighting with their saws trying to take down their trees. I'd wave or nod as I'd walk by and say hi. I never pushed myself on them but I was making it clear I was available if they needed help. I saw a few folks checking out my saw but one lady in particular was almost stalking me. Eventually she had the courage to come close and I immediately greeted her. She had seen me walking with the saw and had come sought me out for help and I was so happy to give it. She expressed concern for her husband who had been trying for like ten minutes to cut a tree with no luck. She thought he may literally have a heart attack. I said "I'd be glad to help," and followed her back through quite a few rows of trees to where her husband was. He was crumpled around the base of the tree in a sweaty mess fighting with that dull saw. I knew exactly how he felt and was so excited to be able to end his struggling.

He crawled away from the tree. I fired up the saw and in less than two seconds the tree was down. I turned off my saw and set it down, brushed off the sawdust, and stood up. Before I even was fully standing up his wife literally jumped up into my arms with a massive embrace of gratitude. Arms wrapped around my neck, her feet dangling off the ground, and me trying not to topple over onto the saw. Service really is its own reward, but that hug was a nice bonus. It gave me such joy to help them out. In future years I would continue to bring my saw to make it easier to cut down our tree and be available to help others if they wanted it. It was always such a gift to me when someone would accept the help that I could give to them.

Under the Hood

My dad had a '56 Chevy in high school which won a few local car shows. I have a distant memory of seeing a photo of it and would have loved to see it in the physical. Neither one of us are "car guys" because that's just too small a label to squeeze into but that doesn't stop me from appreciating a sweet ride when I see one. And boy o' boy was that a sweet ride. I obviously never saw his actual car but I've seen other '56s in movies, photos, and car shows, as well as occasionally in town, which is always exciting. If I could snap my fingers and manifest a car, that would probably be the one. Or maybe the '57 — it'd be a close call. It may have weighed more than today's cars, was perhaps less comfortable to drive, and have had way less safety features but it certainly makes my heart sing to look at it. As do many cars of that era. As the years of safety and fuel efficiency, understandably, took a higher and higher importance we lost style. Maybe it's just me, but everything looks more and more the same every year out there on the road as we've shifted our priorities to safety and comfort. It's interesting what society will give up for comfort.

When my dad and grandfather worked on his car, when he was in high school, my grandfather would often be under the hood doing the main work, as my dad would turn on and off the car, rev up the engine, pump the brakes, or whatever was needed to diagnose the trouble. This was back in the day when you didn't need a Ph.D. in physics to work on a car. You'd open the hood and there it was — the engine! Clearly defined by the empty space around it which also gave you space to move versus today's cars which are packed full and look like a control panel for a spaceship. Without a physics degree one wouldn't dare even begin to look for the spark plugs versus the simple times of diagnosing "Is it spark or is it fuel?" I am well aware of the many benefits to the efficiency in today's cars but for some reason I still hold a place for the simplicity of the past. I guess what's coming to me now is that it's also one less opportunity now for families to connect by tinkering on a car together in the garage. Rather, they just pick up the phone and call a tow truck.

As my grandfather was under the hood looking for whatever the problem was he'd often spot other things that needed attention. Perhaps a loose bolt or screw that could use a little tightening down to make sure it didn't back itself out to the point of falling out. Or maybe one of the fluids looked low so he'd top it off. Perhaps a wire looked frayed so he'd wrap some electrical tape on it. Once he was under the hood, regardless of what had brought him there, he looked at everything. He was looking for other things that could be improved or other areas that might present a problem in the future if not dealt with now. He'd take care of these things without even mentioning it. Often it's a lot easier to fix something before it actually even becomes a problem — nip it in the bud. So what might have started as a simple trip under the hood to tighten a loose spark plug may have also prevented a few other issues as well as provide some bonding time.

My father has used the story of his dad working on his car when he was in high school as an example on and off through the years. Hopefully I have remembered and captured the main pearls of it. The punchline for me has always been to let Prophet, the Comforter, into your heart. It doesn't matter if it's a sweet ride like that '56 Chevy or a VW Beetle. (Also a sweet ride) Once you've invited Prophet in, no matter what the original reason, he's in, and once Prophet is in your heart he can work wonders. Prophet can bring you clarity, healing, wisdom, a greater capacity to give and receive love, guidance on manifesting your purpose, and on and on. There is no downside to opening the hood.

Stay Open

It took a lot of work to clear the spot for our home site, yard, field, and orchard, and now that it's open it requires continued nurturing to keep it open. There is always something creeping in trying to reclaim the space. Always. With the trees gone it allowed for a dramatic increase in light, and with that, life came pouring in. Things that had lain dormant for years stirred. Every tree at the edge of the field now had increased access to the light and leaned in stretching for it versus shooting straight up. For as open and maintained as it is now, if I walked away without handing the weed whacking and chain-sawing torch to somebody else it would be a forest again in a short period of time. To this day, almost twenty years later (at the time of this writing) to the clearing of our home site, if I do not mow the grass for a few weeks I'll have baby trees grow up in the middle of the yard. I have had this happen when my mower has been in the shop for an extended period of time and it always reminds me that if I put down my tools nature would move back in and reclaim my home site to its liking. This really punctuates the point for me that we are all simply visitors here. We're being blessed to experience life in the physical world with its ups and downs, learning more about giving and receiving love in so so many ways, but at the end of the day we are simply visitors. Our true home is the higher heavenly worlds and if we all left Earth someday it would just carry on fine without us. Give it enough time and you'd barely know we had been here. But I say no rush to that ... it's a beautiful place to learn about giving and receiving love. A wonderful training ground for Soul.

All the "heavy lifting" so to say to initially clear my home site was done many years ago but it takes consistent and focused nurturing to keep it open. This goes for helping with the other roads on the property too. If even a single tree or branch falls and blocks the road, it can create the start of a downward cycle, if not cleared, eventually ending in the loss of the road and vehicle access to that part of the property. If it's not cleared and a four-wheeler can no longer pass it gets driven less and less, and if a tractor can no longer drive to do an annual bush hogging and those little trees get bigger and bigger to the point of needing to be chain-sawed eventually heavy equipment needs to be brought back in. More and more effort is required. It just gets beyond the point of easily taking care of and with life being so busy the loss of a road is within the realm of possibility. It's way easier to once a year make a loop with the tractor and bush hog rather than spend a few weeks with a chainsaw, but all that can be messed up by one log across the road. These small blocks make a difference and they can multiply quickly. We've found it best, once one is discovered, to go ahead and make the effort to take care of it as soon as feasible. Make a note of it and as soon as possible head back up with a saw and clear the road — open it up and allow things to get moving again before anything else gets jammed up because of it. A closed road can be the start of a downward spiral.

Even more important than keeping our mountaintop four-wheeler and walking trails open and clear, is keeping our hearts "open" to receive our daily spiritual bread. God whispers guidance, gives support and confidence, expresses His Love for us — His children, and passes on critical insights into every area of our lives, through and to our hearts. Not our physical heart so to say, but the real eternal spiritual being that we are — Soul. Soul cannot receive this guidance clearly though if one's heart is not open. Many things may contribute to these blocks to love, such as fear, worry, anger, or jealousy, just to name a few. If you feel one of these sprouting up it's best to grab the loppers and take care of it before you need that chainsaw — or even better yet, get it when it's small enough to handle with a pair of pruning shears. I like to always have a pair in my back pocket to be ready to nip them in the bud.

The Sandbox

A few years ago we finally downsized our swing set. When in its prime it was glorious to behold and provided hours of solid play. It had a central tower with a platform accessed from a ladder and a canvas roof. Underneath that was a sandbox. Off of that structure were two wings; one was a long monkey bar with a tire swing, rings, and something else. The other extension had all swings. Maxed out at a birthday party that thing was a sight to behold. The girls were grown now and even though they enjoyed it occasionally it wasn't getting enough use to rationalize keeping it any longer. It had also now become a hazard due to its age and solid usage over the years. It was stoutly built, and it took what the girls threw at it like a champ, but nothing wooden that lives out in the wind and the rain lasts forever. The sandbox underneath it didn't help either by holding moisture, which contributed to parts of it rotting. Pieces were now breaking off and nails were starting to make themselves seen. Even patch jobs I had made over the years, where I used screws rather than nails, were starting to fail. The time had come and it was bittersweet. I salvaged what I could and found one new four-by-four so at the end of the day we ended up with a simple small swing set with three swings. It is still satisfying even though it was only a shadow of the original setup and playhouse's glory. We live in the temporal physical world and all things of the flesh must eventually come to an end — even really nice playscapes. Our three little girls had grown into three gorgeous and wonderful young ladies which was the weirdest thing because my wife and I were still the same age as when they were first born. Each one of them is talented and wonderful in their own unique way.

When I took down the swing set I put all the wood scraps in the pile I use for fallen branches over the side of the hill and then I moved all the sand from the large sandbox to a small beach area next to our future pond site. The story of the pond, and trying to get it to hold water could be a parable of its own someday but today is not that day. The next few rains revealed, where I had put the sand, some small pieces of old plastic toys that had nobly lived and died in the sandbox at some point. They had become brittle and the sun had long stolen their color. Seeing them brought back memories of the girls when they were younger and happily playing in the sandbox through the years with various installments of plastic sand toys. It also brought back a memory of how I was initially attached to what kind of toys they were going to have. It's funny when you enter a new venture the picture you have in your head of how it's going to be, even though you may have no clue on the subject, and then how quickly that can all change.

For me it was with our daughter's toys. I don't think it was the first thing I said when I found out we were to be parents but it was an early decree, laid forth with great authority to be upheld from that day forth at all costs. Thou shalt not be any cheap colorful plastic toys in our house or yard. No no no. I will make all our children's toys by hand, all of them ... so saith the future dad. Well that lasted about — well actually that didn't last at all. I think in less than a week or two news had spread we were expecting our first child and gifts of love, in the form of toys, began arriving at the house. And you guessed it — not one of this initial batch was hand carved or made of a natural material. They were quite the contrary. The brightest colors you could possibly imagine in every material imaginable other than natural wood, mostly plastic. Well now, what is a first-time dad who has a head full of ideas on how to raise a kid with nothing to back it up to do ... roll with it I guess, and so I did. These friends and family had expressed their love and well wishes to our new addition in their own way, in a way they thought would make our soon-to-be child happy and they were right. It wasn't what I would have initially picked but I was working with a limited knowledge of the subject. One I had formed from my preferences and not based on any real-world experiences. Our daughter ended up loving most of those gifts and would spend hours with them once she was old enough to actually sit up and play with them. And there were some wooden blocks in the mix, which did get some solid action too, but I must admit she would have missed out on a whole lot of fun without some of that stuff.

When the barnyard animals actually "Mooo and "Cluck" at you, it definitely takes fun to a whole other level.

The toys in the sandbox may not have had the ability to make noise but they made up for it in brightness and color. To think I even considered letting the simple hang-up of "no cheap plastic toys" deny my daughters hours of fun, in the house and outside, is beyond silly but I'm not losing sleep over it. It was what it was. I quickly saw at the time that it was ridiculous and I pivoted — what more can you ask of yourself — do you expect yourself to have it figured out before you even start? I'm not that clever.

What I do need to do is get a head start on making some wooden blocks for potential grandchildren someday. With three daughters it is certainly within the realm of possibility that perhaps one of them will get on an "only wooden toys" kick and actually stick to it. It could be genetic and if so I need a head start, especially if all three do it.

The Rim

It's interesting how we all have pictures in our minds of things we've never seen or experienced for ourselves. The Grand Canyon is a wonderful example of this. When I was growing up I had a pretty solid image of what it was to know the Grand Canyon even though I had myself never been there physically. This picture was built over the years through some incredible photography I had seen, amazing videos and documentaries, as well as speaking with others who had been there and shared their experiences with me. I guess I never really questioned this image I had unconsciously compiled through these secondhand experiences. They had just naturally built over the years one by one into a picture within me of what the "Grand Canyon" was, of what it was like to be familiar with it — to actually know it, to have actually experienced it for myself. I'm not saying I deluded myself into thinking I had actually been there for a visit — that would be cause for concern — rather, I had painted a picture in my head of knowing what it must be like, had I actually visited the Grand Canyon.

Flash forward to the day years later when during a cross-country road trip I walked out onto the rim and beheld it for myself for the first time. All the temporary pictures I had in my mind, or "placeholders," so to say, of what actually was the experience of standing on the rim of the Grand Canyon gazing out across its seemingly endless vastness crumbled. With it came the realization I had been carrying a "black and white" placeholder of sorts of the reality of the canyon — of the experience. One I had compiled through others' memories, snapshots, experiences, and hearsay. This one was actually real — it was mine, and there was no compare. Perhaps the stories served as motivation for me to one day go to see it in person but they ultimately paled in comparison to experiencing it for myself. This realization was so dramatic and tangible. I remember standing there on the rim in awe, literally shaking my head slowly side to side, as the picture I had been carrying for so long shattered. It had unknowingly to me been so lacking and was now completely upgraded with a much higher level of truth and reality.

It had gone from two-dimensional to beyond three-dimensional. I was in it. It was alive. This made me wonder where else in life am I only seeing skin deep — if even that? Where else am I only seeing the "summarized version" I have created of something versus actually experiencing the true reality of it for myself? Where else do I think I already understand something but really have no idea to the fullness, depth, and richness of it? Where else could my life be more? Where else could I experience higher levels of truth?

I remember that day at the Grand Canyon trying to take some photos so I could share with others what I had experienced but realized it was futile. Fragments of its vast beauty could be captured on film or video to a certain degree but not the experience of it. I would not be able to truly share the experience through a photo, I could only use it to inspire someone to make the journey. Those who wanted to know it for themselves would have to make the journey and see it for themselves and experience it for themselves and breathe it in for themselves and be encompassed by it for themselves and bathe in the wonder of it for themselves. All I could do was encourage them to make the journey by sharing how much of a blessing it was for me to make the trip. No one can go to the rim for you. They can tell you about it. They can tell you how glorious it is. They can encourage you. They can inspire you with their stories but we must each ultimately see it for ourselves to truly know it and be blessed by the experience.

And even those who have been to the rim do not see and experience it exactly the same. Everyone who goes there brings back something different. We are each individual spiritual beings created out of love and with love by our Heavenly Father. We have had lifetimes of experience that have helped in giving us our unique view of things. We all see things a little bit differently, and that's a good thing. God loves our uniqueness and He loves when one of His children makes it to a place where they have a higher view. It makes His Heart smile to see one of His children inspired with awe and wonder and love from "the rim" wanting nothing more than to share the view with His other children.

Surrendered to the Echinacea

Not only did our choices in what we planted vary through the years, our effort did as well. Most years we used the entire space but sometimes we'd be busy with other pursuits, such as working on the house, and we'd dial back our time in the garden. Overall though through lots of trial and error we had become pretty proficient at gardening and eventually found with the least amount of effort we could harvest the most amount of fresh produce — even if only using a portion of the beds, which was quite a change from the early years of maximum effort for less return. Food wise, that is ... the joy of the process was always with us regardless of vegetable output.

In the years when we'd only use parts of the garden I'd end up weed whacking the unused portion a few times a year. I always aimed on doing it more to keep the trails in between the beds looking tidy, but life often had something else lined up for me to do and I'd often fall behind on keeping it knocked down. All through this time our two beds of

Echinacea were taking advantage of these lulls in groundskeeping and sending out pioneers to stake claims in new territories. Like the settlers headed to the west coast many years ago these brave seeds traveled far and wide, covering many beds. How they made it such distances from their original home is quite impressive. Initially I would dig them up and plant them in some areas where I wanted new beds but eventually I just kind of let them do their thing. If I saw a nice cluster of them I'd weed whack around it, telling myself, I'll transplant that one later. I eventually did just let them take over half of the garden, and it was one of the most beautiful gardens we had ever had, and I didn't do anything.

In future years I would use these Echinacea plants to transform areas of our yard, that had always been hard to mow, into Echinacea beds. There is now a seemingly endless supply of transplants helping spread what I used to try and contain.

Thinking back to the beginning of my adventure into gardening and my scaled drawing of all the beds, where I'd have every piece of gravel, every weed, every detail completely in control and organized to now letting the Echinacea run free and go where it wanted. It was absolutely gorgeous and I could have never planned it, but my efforts did play a big part in making it happen — just not in the way I could have ever imagined, but all the love we had put into the garden through the years came resounding back. I see such a parallel with our lives when I look at that well-planned and thought-out garden with Echinacea spreading all through it, going where it pleases. Surrendering to the Holy Spirit does not mean just sitting back and saying, "Here I am, do with my life as you want." Quite the opposite. Get up, make plans, have dreams, get your life in gear by making the personal effort to follow them — whatever they may be — but remain open to the suggestions and loving guidance from the Holy Spirit, and then when that gentle whisper comes be okay with the shift and go with it. The suggestion was motivated by love and your life, the lives of your loved ones, and all you come in contact with during your daily walk, will be blessed by it.

Until we Meet Again

Thanks for taking the time to join me on this journey of remembrance and celebration. It was a period in my life of great joy, excitement, growth, love, and simply learning to stand in amazement at the wonder, beauty, and perfection of it all. It is my sincere prayer something I have shared will bring you a moment of joy, laughter, or comfort — perhaps even some peace, or is cause for reflection which brings an insight or understanding that makes your journey through life a little smoother. As I said at the very beginning — you are loved and you are not alone! Nor are you forgotten.

Take care my friends,

Del Hall IV

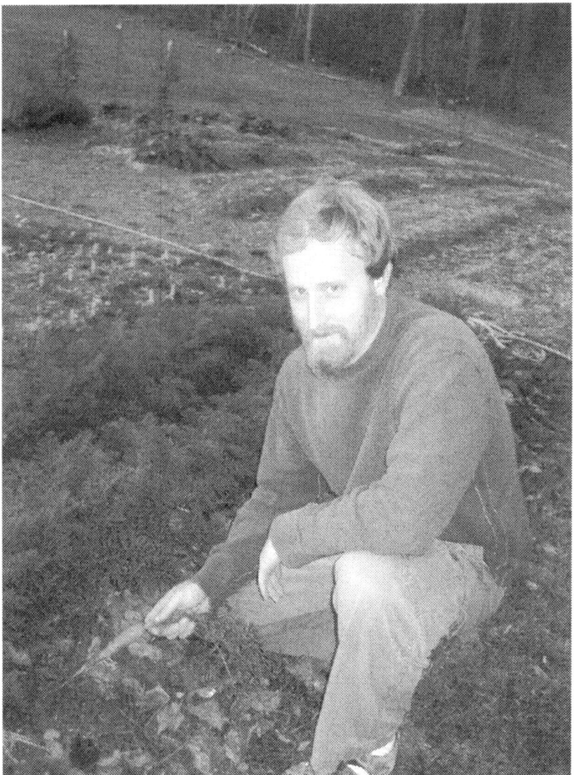